ALTERNATIVE ENERGY SOURCES

REVISED AND UPDATED

science at the edge

SALLY MORGAN

Heinemann Library
Chicago, Illinois

Printed and bound in China by South China Printing Company Ltd.

13 12 11
10 9 8 7 6 5 4 3 2

New edition ISBN: 978 1 4329 2459 1 (hardcover)

The Library of Congress has cataloged the first edition as follows:
Morgan, Sally.
      Alternative energy sources / Sally Morgan.
            v. cm. -- (Science at the edge)
Contents: Fossil fuelled world -- Generating electricity -- Storing energy -- Harnessing the wind -- Trapping light -- Hydro power -- Geothermal power -- Nuclear energy -- Biopower -- The future of renewable sources -- Summary spread -- Time line.
Includes index.
      ISBN 1-40340-322-8   ISBN 978-1-40340-322-3
I. Renewable energy source--Juvenile literature. [I. Renewable energy
      sources. 2. Power resources.] I. Title. II. Series.
TJ808.2 .M67 2002
333.79'4--dc21

Acknowledgments
The author and publishers are grateful to the following for permission to reproduce copyright material:
© Corbis pp. 5 (Darek Delmanowicz/epa), 10 (M. Thomsen/Zefa), 17 (Brooks Kraft), 23 (Gerald French), 28 (George Steinmetz), 33 (Du Huaju/Xinhua Press); © Ecoscene pp. 13 (Joel Creed), 37 (Alexandra Jones), 39 (Peter Hulme), 40 (Kevin King), 55 (Andrew Brown), 35, 46, 47, 51, 52, 56; © Getty Images p. 27 (Popperfoto); © Middelgrundens Vindmøllelaug p. 20; © NASA p. 31; © Photolibrary Group pp. 19 (OSF), 29 (Japan Travel Bureau), 49 (Photononstop); © Photoshot p. 48 (Bloomberg News/Landov); © Reuters p. 24 (Popperfoto); © Science Photo Library pp. 7 (Alex Bartel), 8 (Tony Craddock), 11 (Vanessa Vick), 21, 32, 36 (Martin Bond), 25 (Peter Menzel), 38 (John Mead), 43 (Novosti), 44 (US Department of Energy and Science), 45 (Los Alamos National Laboratory), 50 (Prof David Hall), 15.

Cover photograph of solar panels reproduced with permission of © Corbis/Roger Ressmeyer.

Every effort has been made to contact copyright holders of any material reproduced in this book. Any omissions will be rectified in subsequent printings if notice is given to the publisher.

CONTENTS

Some words are printed in bold, **like this**. You can find
out what they mean by looking in the glossary.

INTRODUCTION

During 2001 the residents of California discovered what it would be like to live in a world where **electricity** was in short supply. In that year there were periods of time when the supply could not keep up with the demand. Entire districts had to survive without electricity for many hours. This crisis was caused by a change in the way the power companies sold **energy,** but is good example of how people have become dependent on a regular supply of electricity.

One of the immediate effects of the crisis was that many Californians turned to alternative energy sources. People rushed out and bought solar panels to provide their homes with electricity and hot water. This gave them independence from the electricity companies that had traditionally provided their energy.

Run on Fossil Fuels

The modern world is dependent on **fossil fuels**—oil, gas, coal, and peat. Over the last 200 years or so, the quantities of fossil fuels extracted from the ground have escalated. Fossil fuels are used by power plants to generate electricity and fuel cars. They are essential to a modern lifestyle, but they have been used at the expense of the environment.

Environmental damage is caused at every stage of extracting, processing, and using fossil fuels. Coal is mined from the ground, while oil and gas are pumped out of the ground. Then they have to be transported around the world to where they will be used. Finally, when they are burned, these fuels release polluting gases into the atmosphere and cause **acid rain** and **global warming**.

The supply of fossil fuels will eventually run out. Estimates of how long these fuels will last are uncertain because new deposits are being found all the time. However, most experts agree that oil and gas will probably last between 30 and 100 years, while coal may last 200 years.

Concerns about supplies of fossil fuels and rising energy prices are common around the world. These trucks have stopped at the Polish-Ukrainian border as part of a one-hour protest against rising fuel prices in 2008.

New Energy Sources

Over a number of years, people have learned how to use the energy locked in fossil fuels. But there are other sources of energy, too. Each day, vast amounts of solar energy reach the ground. This energy is spread over the whole surface of the planet. The same is true for wind and wave energy. These forms of energy are currently more difficult and expensive to use than fossil fuels. However, when fossil fuels start to run out, people will need to find ways to use the energy from these **renewable** sources. At some point in the future, the world's energy needs will probably have to come from these sources.

A FOSSIL-FUELED WORLD

Although there are many different sources of energy available, more than 75 percent of the energy used in industrialized countries comes from oil, gas, and coal. These fuels are rich in carbon and hydrogen. They burn to form carbon dioxide and water, a process that releases heat energy.

Fossil Fuel Supplies

Fossil fuels were formed millions of years ago from the remains of plants and animals. There is a limited supply of these fuels. They are now being used up at a far faster rate than they are being formed. Soon, they will run out.

DRILLING FOR OIL

Oil is formed under the ocean from the remains of marine life. The oil formation process is similar to that of coal (see below). The remains become buried under layers of sediment, and the resulting high pressure and temperature cause them to turn into a black liquid with a high carbon content. Often, gas forms in the same place as the oil. The liquid oil moves toward the surface and becomes trapped under layers of **impermeable** rock. The pressure builds up as more liquid moves upward.

Although oil is formed under the ocean, many of the world's oil fields are on land. This is a result of changes in sea levels and movements on Earth that have uplifted rocks, causing them to lie above water.

FOCUS Coal Formation

The process of coal formation starts with a buildup of dead plant matter, which becomes buried in swampy or waterlogged conditions. The lack of oxygen in the ground prevents bacteria from completely breaking down the plant matter. This decaying matter is buried deeper by more plant material and by sediment. These layers press tightly together, causing the pressure and temperature to increase. Gases and liquids escape to the surface, leaving a solid material behind. Peat develops within hundreds of years and contains about 60 percent carbon. Millions of years later, the peat turns into lignite, a low-grade brown coal that is 70 percent carbon. Eventually, the lignite turns into anthracite coal. This is a high-quality coal that is 95 percent carbon.

Oil and gas are reached by drilling wells, sometimes several miles deep, through the overlying rock. When the drill breaks through the rock above the oil, pressure is released, and the oil spurts out of the well. To prevent this from happening, engineers place special valves at the top of the well. When there is not enough pressure to push the oil to the surface, water or gas can be pumped into the well to force the oil out.

The **crude oil** that comes out must be taken to refineries, where it is processed before it can be used.

Oil companies are now searching for new oil and gas fields in some of the world's most inhospitable places, such as the frozen ice fields of Siberia and Alaska and the Arctic Ocean. Once all the oil fields are depleted, the energy companies may turn their attention to oil shales. These are rocks that have oil inside them. However, removing oil from rock is very expensive and produces a lot of waste.

A nodding donkey rig pumps oil to the surface at an onshore oil field in California.

Fossil Fuels and Air Pollution

Fossil fuels produce a number of **pollutants** when they are burned, in addition to carbon dioxide and water. Coal often contains sulfur, which is released as sulfur dioxide—one of the chemicals that cause acid rain. When gasoline and diesel fuel are burned in engines, gases such as nitrous oxide and carbon monoxide are released.

SMOG

Gases and particles from car **exhaust** pipes can create photochemical **smog**. This form of smog is common in hot, dry, sunny cities, such as Athens in Greece, Cairo in Egypt, and Mexico City. Car exhaust pipes in these places pump out gases, such as nitrous oxide and carbon monoxide, that react together in the sunlight. The result is a smoggy haze over the city.

Los Angeles, California, has suffered badly in the past from smog. The smog was due in part to the exhaust fumes from millions of cars, but the local geography also played a role. The city lies by the coast and is surrounded by mountains. In certain weather conditions, the smoggy air would become trapped over the city. Air quality would fall steadily, until atmospheric conditions changed and the smoggy air was replaced by cleaner air. A hazy layer can still be seen over Los Angeles, but the level of pollutants has fallen dramatically due to new legislation and improved pollution controls in cars.

A deep photochemical smog can clearly be seen over the city of Hong Kong in China. Various emissions from motor vehicles react with low-level ozone to form this brown, hazy smog. High levels of smog pose a serious health hazard, especially to the elderly, the very young, or those with existing respiratory problems.

ACID RAIN

Coal-fired power plants release sulfur dioxide, especially those that burn lignite coal. Sulfur dioxide, together with nitrous oxide released from vehicle exhausts, reacts with water in the air to form weak acids. These acids create acid rain. Acid rain has a lower **pH** than normal. It erodes and damages the outsides of buildings and statues, especially those made of limestone.

Acid rain falling on conifer forests in mountainous areas of Scandinavia, North America, and central Europe has caused long-term damage to the trees. The soil becomes more acidic, and this causes toxic compounds, such as aluminum, to be released. The first signs of damage are a tree's needles turning brown and whole branches dying. Increased acidity in the soil damages the roots, reducing the tree's ability to take up water and nutrients. Trees become more vulnerable to frost and disease. Eventually, they die.

Lakes are also at risk. Acidic rainwater drains off the soil into the lake, causing it to become more acidic. Aluminum in the water causes the gills of fish to produce more mucus, and this prevents them from obtaining sufficient oxygen from the water. In extreme cases, all life in the water may die.

 FOCUS **Fossil Fuels and Global Warming**

Burning fossil fuels releases carbon dioxide. Carbon dioxide is described as a greenhouse gas because it traps heat in the atmosphere. The presence of some greenhouse gases keeps Earth at a temperature of approximately 15°C (59°F), which allows life to survive. A recent increase in the use of fossil fuels has caused the level of carbon dioxide in the atmosphere to increase, too. More carbon dioxide means that more heat is trapped, and this has caused the average global temperature to rise. This is called global warming.

The effects of global warming are uncertain, but they are predicted to be many and catastrophic. Increasing temperatures may disrupt climates around the world, causing some regions to have lower rainfall and others to have more. The warmer temperatures have already caused ice caps and glaciers to melt. This is causing sea levels to rise, flooding low-lying areas that are heavily populated. Extreme weather events, such as droughts and storms, are also becoming more common.

Extracting and Transporting Fossil Fuels

Every stage in extracting and processing fossil fuels can harm the environment. Coal is either mined from the surface, in huge opencast mines (also called strip mines), or by underground tunnels. Opencast mining destroys land and leaves behind huge holes of little use that send dust and other debris into the atmosphere. Lignite is a poor-quality coal that is taken from opencast mines. When burned, it releases sulfur dioxide, which creates acid rain. Mining produces large quantities of waste, which is usually dumped in piles (called spoil heaps). Water runs off these heaps, and the drainage from these areas can carry pollutants into rivers and lakes.

Wells are dug into the ground to bring oil to the surface. There can be local damage from oil spills, but most of damage occurs during the transportation of oil. Some of the largest ocean tankers carry up to 500,000 metric tons of crude oil and many only have a single hull. Any damage to the hull results in an oil spill. In the past there have been numerous tanker accidents in which hundreds of thousands of tons of crude oil have been spilt into oceans. The oil causes widespread damage to local populations of birds, mammals, and invertebrates, and also damages coastlines. Large quantities of oil also enter the water when tankers are cleaned or minor spills occur in ports.

Garzweiler in Germany is a huge brown-coal opencast mine.

In 1989 the oil tanker *Exxon Valdez* ran aground off the coast of Alaska and its tanks were ruptured. The disaster created a huge oil slick and terrible environmental damage. The cleanup operation cost billions of dollars.

FOCUS   Why Do Increasing Energy Demands Call for Change?

Energy demands are increasing all the time. Approximately 25 percent of the world's population lives without electricity, 80 percent of whom live in areas of sub-Saharan Africa and southern Asia. They rely solely on battery power and **kerosene** lamps and candles. Governments want to supply these people with electricity in order to improve their standard of living. To do so would mean building thousands of new power plants in order to increase the current energy-generating capacity. This would greatly reduce the remaining supplies of fossil fuels and send carbon dioxide emissions out of control.

The way forward is to instead use renewable sources of energy, which provide electricity without causing great damage to the environment. At the same time, people will have to use fossil fuels more efficiently to ensure that the supply lasts as long as possible—cars will have to travel farther using a smaller amount of gasoline and power plants will need to be more **efficient**.

MAKING AND STORING ELECTRICITY

The electricity generation process involves a number of energy changes, regardless of the initial source. Traditionally, electricity was generated using coal. More recently, power plants have used other fossil fuels, such as oil and gas, as their energy source. Oil-fired power plants are common in oil-producing countries, such as Indonesia. Gas burns more cleanly and efficiently than coal—releasing half as much carbon dioxide and more than 1,000 times less sulfur dioxide per unit of energy.

Burning Fossil Fuels in Power Plants

The heat released from burning fossil fuels is used to boil water, which produces steam. The steam is then heated to high temperatures, which increases its pressure so it can turn huge steam **turbines**. Some of the energy of the steam is transformed into movement, or **kinetic energy**, as the turbines spin. The turbines are connected to the coils of large **generators**. The coils carry a **current** and act as **electromagnets**. As the turbines spin, they produce an electric current in the fixed coils surrounding them. This is fed into a power supply grid and carried to wherever it is needed.

Power plants cannot store surplus electricity, so electricity generation has to match demand. The electric companies have to estimate how much power will be needed. During periods of hot weather, electricity demand may increase because more people use air conditioning to keep their homes and offices cool. If electric companies' estimates are wrong, people may experience power cuts.

Power plants are not very efficient. Between 50 and 70 percent of the energy contained in fossil fuels is wasted. Some of the heat energy heats the surrounding air and escapes through boiler chimneys. Not all the heat energy locked in the steam can be transferred to the spinning turbines. Although the steam is cooler when it leaves than when it enters the turbines, it is still warm. The steam is carried to cooling towers, where it cools sufficiently to **condense** back into water. The warm water is then emptied into a nearby river or sea, where it can cause thermal (heat) pollution.

Warm water holds less oxygen than cold water. The addition of a large quantity of warm water to rivers, lakes, or oceans can be fatal to some animals. For example, fish can suffocate because they are unable to extract enough oxygen from the water.

COMBINED HEAT AND POWER PLANTS

Some power plants, known as combined heat and power plants (CHPs), try to make use of waste heat. They send waste hot water through pipes to surrounding businesses and homes to provide heating. There are many units like this in Germany, and many small towns benefit from this cheap energy source. However, this is only possible in small and medium-sized power plants that are built close to towns. In many countries, power plants are located in remote locations, so this energy source is not practical.

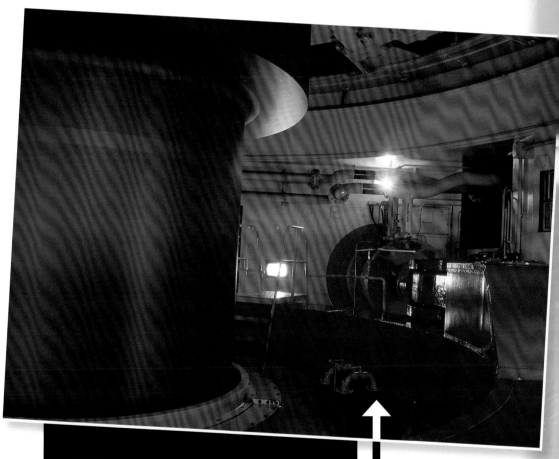

Unlike fossil fuels, water is a renewable source of energy. This turbine room at the Itaipu Dam in Brazil uses falling water, not steam, to spin the turbines and produce electricity.

Storing Energy

Electricity is usually generated at a level that meets demand because it is difficult to store surplus energy. However, it is possible to store small amounts of energy for personal and domestic uses. Batteries and **fuel cells** both produce electricity by using **electrochemical** reactions. **Flywheels** store energy as they spin.

THE BATTERY

A convenient store of energy is the electric cell, or battery. Batteries are used every day to power flashlights, radios, toys, and many other things. The most common form of battery contains carbon and zinc, separated by a solution of ammonium chloride. When a battery is connected to an electrical circuit, its stored chemical energy is changed into electrical energy. The battery continues to produce an electric current until all the chemicals have reacted with each other. Then, the battery is said to be dead. Batteries containing nickel and cadmium (Nicads) can be recharged by passing a small electric current through the battery for several hours. This makes them last much longer.

FLYWHEELS

Space stations use **photovoltaic panels** and fuel cells as their source of energy. This energy is stored in batteries. These batteries are large and expensive and have to be replaced every five years. But many of the latest space stations and **satellites** use flywheels to store the energy. These can last up to 20 years. Flywheels are used in engines, but now scientists are designing even more efficient types of flywheels. When energy is used to spin a flywheel, the energy is converted to kinetic energy. The faster the flywheel spins, the more energy it stores.

FOCUS Powered by Air

When air is pumped into a tire, it becomes compressed and is under great pressure. When the tire valve is released, the air rushes out with some force. This idea could be used on a much larger scale by power plants. When a power plant produces too much electricity, it is usually wasted. Some of this surplus electricity could be used to pump air into underground chambers, such as old salt mines, oil wells, or even natural caves. The surplus electricity would be used to force the air into the chamber under pressure. When the demand for electricity became high, this trapped air could be released to power air-driven turbines.

This energy can be converted to electricity. Newer flywheels will be just 15 centimeters (6 inches) across and made of extremely strong, yet lightweight, materials. They will spin up to 600,000 times each minute and store eight times more energy than a battery of the same mass.

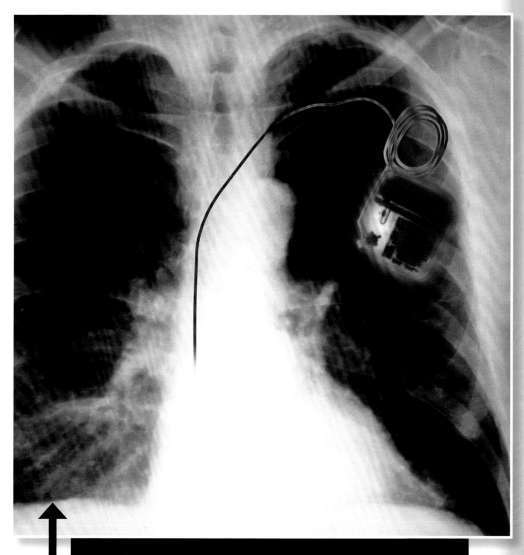

An artificial heart pacemaker is made of titanium and contains a tiny generator powered by batteries. The batteries are designed for the highly specialized job of keeping the heart beating at the right speed. The pacemaker is inserted under the skin of the chest wall and is connected to the heart. The batteries last a long time and can be changed under local anesthetic.

Fuel Cells

Fuel cells date back to 1839. Until quite recently, only the U.S. National Aeronautics and Space Administration (NASA) made use of them. However, fuel cells are now becoming more common and are used in vehicles and buildings to provide power.

All fuel cells are energy converters and work on the same basic principle. They have two **electrodes** separated by an **electrolyte**, a substance that conducts electricity. A fuel, such as hydrogen, enters at one electrode, and oxygen enters at the other. They undergo a reaction, which produces an electric current. When the fuel used is hydrogen, the only waste product is pure water.

Fuel cells have many advantages. They convert energy far more efficiently than conventional power sources. For example, a fuel cell is twice as efficient as a car engine run on gasoline and produces virtually no pollution. Furthermore, fuel cells contain no moving parts, so do not produce any noise or vibration. An operating fuel cell is, therefore, very quiet and does not suffer from wear and tear. However, there are a number of problems to overcome. Fuel cells are expensive. Today, more fuel cells are being manufactured, so the price is falling. There are also problems of reliability with some fuel cells. In addition, some larger fuel cells have poor power-to-weight and power-to-volume ratios. This means that for their weight or volume, they produce relatively small amounts of power.

> *"There's no other technology around like fuel cells. They are basically black boxes, you put fuel in one end and get electricity out the other, with great fuel efficiency and low emissions."*
>
> Edward Gillis, Electric Power Research Institute, California

USING FUEL CELLS

Fuel cells are already being used in some buses in differnt cities, including London and Amsterdam. The fuel cell works with an electric motor that converts the electrical power from the fuel cell into a force to turn the wheels. The first fuel cell-powered cars are now appearing, too. These cars are emission-free, so ideal for places such as California, which has strict emission laws. Larger fuel cell systems are being tested in small power plants and in houses. A police station in Central Park, New York, is using a large fuel cell to provide its electricity and heating. It cost more than $1 million to install, but this was cheaper than having

A hydrogen fuel cell vehicle fills up at the first hydrogen dispenser at a gas station in the United States. As an alternative fuel source, hydrogen has zero emissions and gets two to three times the mileage of traditional gasoline. Major car manufacturers, such as General Motors, are developing fuel cell technologies and consumer lines of hydrogen cars targeted for mass production by 2010.

to lay electricity cables across the park. One of the huge, illuminated signs in Times Square, New York, is also powered by electricity produced by fuel cells. Hundreds of similar fuel cells have been sold around the world. They are ideal for places that are too remote to be on the national power grid, such as Alaska. Smaller cells are being developed as alternatives to a household water heater.

HYDROGEN FUEL CELLS

Although fuel cells can be run on a number of fuels, the cleanest is hydrogen. Hydrogen can be obtained from a number of sources. Currently, 90 percent of hydrogen comes from natural gas (a fossil fuel) so is, in fact, not a fossil fuel replacement. Hydrogen can also be obtained from organic wastes, a renewable source, or by a process called electrolysis. Electrolysis involves passing an electric current through acidic water, which splits it into oxygen and hydrogen. This method uses a lot of electricity, but in the future could be generated from renewable energy sources, such as wind or solar energy.

HARNESSING THE WIND

Wind turbines are becoming an increasingly common sight. Traditionally, wind turbines were built to pump water. Though many still carry out this function, more are being built to generate electricity. Worldwide, wind power generating capacity has recently been growing by about 30 percent per year. In 2007 the total generating capacity reached just under 100 **gigawatts** (equivalent to the amount generated by 25 large power plants fired by fossil fuels). Other than during the manufacture and installation of turbines, generating power from wind uses no fuel and does not produce harmful emissions or waste. Today, millions of people are supplied with clean, renewable electricity from the wind.

Windy Locations

Wind turbines are built in places that are windy all the time, such as along coasts and the shores of some large lakes. The modern wind turbine has a tall tower with two or three blades at the top. The blades are moved by the wind. A spinning generator directly converts the kinetic energy into electricity.

WIND TURBINE DESIGN

Wind turbines come in two basic designs. The key difference is in the drive shaft. This is the part of the turbine that connects the blades to the generator. The most common design is the horizontal axis turbine, which has two or three blades. Horizontal axis turbines have a horizontal drive shaft.

Vertical axis turbines have vertical drive shafts. The blades are long, curved, and attached to the tower at the top and bottom. There are also shrouded wind turbines that have a hood around the rotor. This funnels the wind, causing it to move faster over the blades and spin them more quickly.

The higher above ground wind turbines are placed, the stronger the wind. With this in mind, recent turbines have been built bigger and taller than before. The extra height ensures the blades are spun by faster-moving air. Building one large turbine is cheaper than building a lot of small ones. The tallest turbines stand at about 140 meters (260 feet). One of the world's largest turbines even has blades that are 60 meters (197 ft.) long! Turbines need to survive gusty winds, so they are built from light and strong **composite** materials.

THE LAYOUT

The placing of the wind turbines is also important. If they are too close together, they block the wind from neighbouring turbines. Computers are used to work out the best positions. Electronic monitors measure the wind speed and direction. This information is used to adjust the angle of the blades and the direction of the whole turbine to suit the wind conditions. If the blades were allowed to spin too fast, they could break. If the wind is too strong, the blades are either turned out of the wind, or brakes are applied.

"Wind power is increasingly economically competitive with conventional sources of electricity. Increasing volatility in fossil fuel prices and increased concerns about energy security mean that wind power is often the most attractive option for new generation capacity, from any point of view."

Professor Arthouros Zervos, chairperson of the Global Wind Energy Council, 2007

The Tehachapi-Mojave wind farm is located in the Mojave Desert in California.

Middelgrunden Offshore Wind Farm

The largest offshore wind farm in the world was built outside Copenhagen harbor in Denmark. There are 20 wind generators there, situated in water 3–5 meters (10–16 ft.) deep. Each generator is 63 meters (207 ft.) tall, with 36.8-meter (121-ft.) blades. The generators are 180 meters (591 ft.) apart, stretching in an arc for 3.4 kilometers (2 miles). The turbines generate enough electricity to power three percent of Copenhagen's energy needs each year.

Before the wind farm was constructed, the power company did an environmental impact assessment. The wind farm was to be built on a former dump for harbor waste, so the area was classified as unclean. The assessment evaluated what effect the wind farm would have on local bird and fish populations, what impact the dredging and construction operation would have, and what the visual impact would be. It concluded that there would be no adverse impact on the area. It is estimated that the wind farm will result in annual savings of 258 metric tons of sulfur dioxide, 76,000 metric tons of carbon dioxide, 231 metric tons of nitrogen oxides, and 4,900 metric tons of dust, compared with generating the same amount of electricity using fossil fuels.

The 20 wind generators of the Middelgrunden wind farm have been built in shallow water just off Copenhagen in Denmark.

DISCUSS

Are Wind Farms a Scar on the Landscape and a Threat to Wildlife?

There is no doubt that generating electricity using wind power is clean. However, many people are against this source of energy because of the large number of wind turbines that must be built in rural areas and off coastlines. People complain that wind farms are unattractive and noisy. In the past, wind farms did generate noise from the swishing of the blades and the hum of the gearbox. Modern designs, however, have eliminated most of the noise. Many people think that a wind farm makes a landscape more interesting, but there are just as many who think that a wind farm is unattractive. What do you think?

There is considerable disturbance during the construction of a wind farm, with new access roads and the digging of foundations that extend deep into the ground. Once constructed, the land around the turbines can be used as before—for livestock grazing, for example. But cables must be laid to connect to the main electricity grid and this can be destructive if the wind farm is in a remote location.

There is also concern that the rotating blades of a wind farm could harm local bird populations. In California, some of the early wind farms were built in areas of high conservation value, and birds were injured. There have also been reports of birds, such as eagles and migrating storks, being killed by the blades. Location and modern turbine design can reduce this risk. The blades of the largest turbines spin more slowly (about one rotation every five seconds) so are easier for birds to see. Birds can even nest in turbines with lattice, rather than solid, towers. Besides, more birds are killed from flying into buildings and power lines, or being hit by cars, than by flying into spinning blades.

A row of wind turbines stretches across an attractive area of Anglesey, Wales. Many people consider this wind farm to be intrusive and unattractive on the landscape. What do you think?

Around the World

Although Europe and North America lead the way with the number of wind turbines, other places are rapidly catching up. India holds fourth place, with a total wind power capacity of 8,000 **megawatts** in size. China has more than 6,000 megawatts. There are many small-scale projects in the less economically developed regions of the world. In these places, for example, on small Pacific Islands and in some mountain communities, wind power can provide remote villages with an electricity source. The number of offshore wind turbines is increasing, too. They currently account for just under two percent of total wind power, but this is increasing every year.

TUMBLING COSTS

Until 2004 the cost of building new wind farms was decreasing. Between 1990 and 2002 wind energy capacity doubled every three years, and building costs fell by 15 percent. Since 2004, oil, gas, and coal prices have more than tripled. This has pushed electricity prices up. There have also been recent rises in the cost of building materials, especially steel, aluminum, and copper, which are all used to construct towers and conventional power plants.

Wind for the Future

The outlook for wind energy looks extremely promising, especially as wind turbines become increasingly efficient at converting wind energy into electricity. If the current rate of growth continues, the total wind power capacity worldwide could reach 2,000 gigawatts by the year 2020. With sufficient encouragement, it could even reach as much as 3,000 gigawatts—30 times the amount of wind power available in 2008.

DISCUSS   The Wind Farm Debate

There is much debate about whether or not wind farms are environmentally friendly and energy saving. Those opposed to wind farms claim that each turbine needs up to 1,000 metric tons of concrete in its foundations and that this, together with the energy cost of building new roads and laying cables, uses up more energy than the turbine will produce in its 20-year lifetime. The supporters of wind farms say that the energy used in construction takes no more than five months to pay back, and that this energy return is far better than it would be if building a new coal-fired power plant.

This wind farm is in Palm Springs, California.

TRAPPING LIGHT

The Sun is a source of both light and heat energy. The heat energy can be used to heat air and water. The light energy can be used to generate electricity. One of the major advantages of **solar power** is that this free source of energy can be used in remote locations.

Solar Collectors

Solar collectors trap the Sun's heat energy. A solar collector consists of a large, flat glass-covered box that contains a dark, metal plate. The plate absorbs the heat, and the glass stops it from escaping. Air or water flowing through a tube at the bottom of the box is warmed by the heat. Solar collectors are used to heat homes, provide hot water and air conditioning, produce salt, and turn saltwater into fresh drinking water in a process called desalination.

Photovoltaics

Solar cells, which use a technology known as photovoltaics, can convert light energy into electrical energy. Photovoltaic power centers were originally developed for use in space, where they could make use of a free source of energy—the Sun. They still power most satellites circling Earth because they operate reliably for long periods and require virtually no maintenance.

Panels of photovoltaic cells, such as those that circle this lighthouse off the coast of Guernsey in the Channel Islands, are a useful source of electricity in remote places.

Photovoltaic power systems do not burn fuel and have no moving parts, so they are clean and silent. This is especially important when the main alternatives for obtaining power and light in remote places are diesel generators and kerosene lanterns and candles. Once installed, photovoltaic power systems can operate continuously, with little upkeep and low operating costs.

Photovoltaic cells are small, so they are easy to transport to remote places to produce electricity. For example, a few panels about 1 meter (3 ft.) in height are sufficient to power communication stations on mountain tops, or navigational buoys in the ocean. Buildings can have special roofs made of photovoltaic panels, which generate electricity for use within the building. Photovoltaics can generate electricity to pump water, charge batteries, and run weather stations. Tiny photovoltaic cells are also found in some pocket calculators.

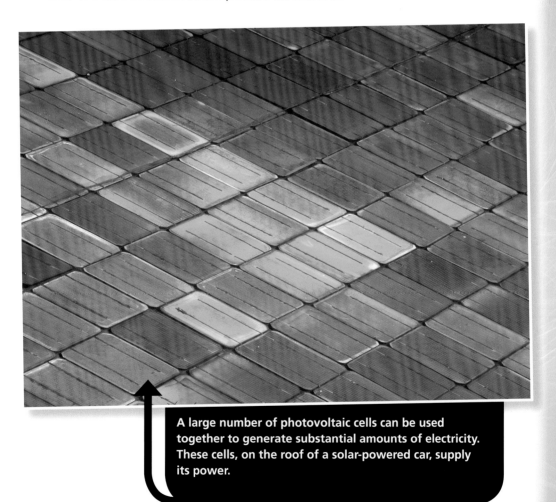

A large number of photovoltaic cells can be used together to generate substantial amounts of electricity. These cells, on the roof of a solar-powered car, supply its power.

INSIDE A CELL

The most important parts of a photovoltaic cell are the thin layers of silicon inside it. Silicon is a **semiconductor**. When light hits the cell, electrical charges move between the layers and produce an electric current. The more light there is, the more electricity that can be produced. A glass cover or similar transparent material seals the cell and keeps rain out. A nonreflective coating prevents light from being reflected away from the cell.

The proportion of sunlight energy that the photovoltaic cell converts to electric energy is called conversion efficiency. Improving this efficiency is one way to make solar energy competitive with more traditional sources of energy. The first photovoltaic cells converted just one or two percent of sunlight energy into electrical energy. The latest cells have a conversion efficiency of up to 33 percent. This means they can be used in places where it is not sunny all the time.

As more photovoltaic cells are manufactured, the cost of making them will come down. Already, the latest photovoltaic cells are produced at a fraction of the cost of early photovoltaic systems. In time, the cost of producing electricity from photovoltaic cells will be competitive with the cost of electricity produced using fossil fuels.

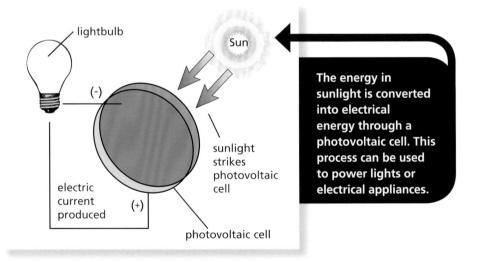

lightbulb

Sun

(-)

The energy in sunlight is converted into electrical energy through a photovoltaic cell. This process can be used to power lights or electrical appliances.

sunlight strikes photovoltaic cell

electric current produced

(+)

photovoltaic cell

"There's an emerging market in the automobile industry—using photovoltaic products on the sunroof. A number of manufacturers are considering photovoltaics to ventilate a car—running a fan to keep the air moving when an auto sits in a parking lot."

John Corsi, chief executive officer of Solarex (solar panel manufacturers)

In 2001 NASA ran test flights on its Helios prototype. This unmanned flying wing runs on solar power. The entire top surface of the wing is covered with solar panels. Helios can cruise for days at altitudes three times higher than those used by commercial jets.

FOCUS New Research: Quantum Dots

The efficiency of converting sunlight into electricity could be pushed up to 65 percent by using nanotechnology. Nanotechnology is engineering at a molecular level, building structures from single atoms and molecules. When light strikes a photovoltaic cell, electrical charges in the cell are given more energy. This causes the charges to jump between the layers of silicon. It is this movement that generates electricity. Usually, one photon of light boosts the energy of one electric charge. Nanocrystals, called quantum dots, boost up to three electric charges from one photon of light. If this technology is used in photovoltaic cells, they could generate far more electricity.

Solar Power Plants

Solar power plants have been built in sunny locations such as California and Israel. There are two main types of solar power plants. Solar thermal power plants use sunlight to heat a fluid, which in turn heats water, to produce steam. Photovoltaic power plants use photovoltaic cells to convert sunlight into electricity.

Work started on the first solar thermal power plant, Solar One, near Barstow, California, in the late 1970s. Electricity was first generated there in 1982. More than 1,800 mirrors were laid out in semicircles around a 78-meter (256-ft.) tower. The mirrors directed sunlight onto a boiler at the top of the tower. As the Sun moved through the sky, the mirrors followed it. Oil in the central collecting tower was heated and piped to a power plant. There, it heated water to 3,000°C (5,432°F) to produce steam. The steam was used to spin a turbine, which drove a generator to produce 10 **kilowatts** of electricity.

Other power plants have mirrors shaped like feed troughs, which reflect sunlight onto a tube at the bottom. The Luz plant in California uses this mirror shape. A liquid inside the tube is heated by sunlight.

The world's most technically advanced solar power facility, Solar Two, in Daggit, California, focuses the Sun's rays on a tower containing liquid salt. This is then pumped into an insulated tank so that stored heat can drive turbines and provide electric power 24 hours a day.

In remote areas, solar energy can be used as a source of heat for cooking and boiling water. The heat from these makeshift solar panels is used to boil water in this kettle.

During the last 10 years, an emphasis has been put on building power plants that use photovoltaic cells, especially thin-film solar cells (see page 30). Many solar power plants have opened, each larger than the previous one.

In 2008 the world's largest photovoltaic power plant opened in eastern Portugal. This area of Portugal receives the most annual sunlight in terms of area in Europe, so was the perfect place to build a plant. The plant consists of 2,520 giant solar panels. The panels are located on a hillside. Each one tracks the Sun during the day, supplying 45 megawatts of electricity per year. Portugal has no natural fossil fuel supplies or nuclear power plants, so it has decided to use renewable energy sources instead.

"We have to reduce our dependence on oil and gas. What seemed extravagant in 2004 when we decided to go for renewables now seems to have been a very good decision."

Manuel Pinho, economics minister, Portugal, 2008

In 2008 other solar power plants being planned included one to supply 45,000 homes in Victoria, Australia. Another, near Phoenix, Arizona, would generate 280 megawatts of electricity to power 80,000 homes.

Thin-Film Technology

The latest generation of solar cells do not use silicon. Instead, new thin-film cells are based on a semiconductor containing copper, indium, gallium, and selenide (referred to as CIGS). The thin-film panels are actually printed onto a flexible backing sheet. This makes them suitable for putting on windows, mobile phones, the sides of buildings, and even clothing.

One of the major disadvantages of the more conventional silicon photovoltaic cells is their cost. They are so expensive that they take many years to pay for themselves. Manufacturing them also uses a lot of energy and involves chemical processes. Although the efficiency of a thin-film cell is only about 10 percent, it is much cheaper to manufacture than a silicon cell. Once thin-film cells are commercially available, the price of generating solar power could fall from about $4 per watt to less than 60 cents per watt within 10 years.

 FOCUS **Solar Paint**

Researchers at Swansea University in Wales are investigating the possibility of painting solar cells onto steel surfaces. Observations showing how sunlight degrades paint led to the idea that maybe the paint itself could capture solar energy. In order to do this, sheets of steel would be passed through rollers and many layers of solar paint would be applied. Light falling on the solar paint could then be captured and used to generate electricity. If this process proves to be successful, solar paint would be good for use in places with less sunny climates, such as Britain, because research shows it should work well in low light conditions.

"Corus Colors produces around 100 million square meters of steel building cladding a year. If this was treated with the photovoltaic material, and assuming a conservative five percent energy conversion rate, then we could be looking at generating 4,500 gigawatts of electricity through the solar cells, annually. That's the equivalent output of roughly 50 wind farms."

Dr. David Worsley, Materials Research Center at the University of Swansea's School of Engineering, Wales

Orbiting Solar Power Plants

Japan's Ministry of Economy, Trade, and Industry (METI) has announced plans to launch a giant solar power plant by the year 2040. METI wants to launch a satellite capable of generating 1 million kilowatts per second, equivalent to the output of a nuclear power plant. The satellite would enter orbit about 36,000 km (22,370 miles) above Earth's surface and would have two huge, solar power-generating wing panels.

Each panel would be 3 km (1.9 miles) long, with power transmission antenna measuring 1,000 meters (3,282 ft.) between them. The electricity would be sent to Earth in the form of microwaves. The receiving antenna, on the ground in a desert or in the ocean, would have a diameter of several miles. The electricity would be relayed from the receiving antenna along cables. The satellite is projected to weigh about 20,000 metric tons. The total construction cost is expected to be the equivalent of tens of billions of dollars. The estimated cost of generating power in space is high compared with thermal or nuclear power generation, but this may change as the technology improves.

An artist's impression of a solar power plant shows the wings of a satellite covered with solar panels.

"On Earth, clouds absorb sunlight, reducing [solar] power generation. But in space, we will be able to generate electric power even at night."

Osamu Takenouchi, METI

WATER POWER

Water can provide power in many different ways. Hydroelectric plants involve building a dam across a river to create a storage area for water that can then be released through turbines to generate electricity. Ocean wave and tidal power can also be used to generate electricity.

Hydroelectric Power

In 2006 hydroelectric power provided about 19 percent of the world's electricity. It is an important source of energy in mountainous areas and less economically developed countries. The Itaipu Dam in Brazil is the largest hydroelectric power source, but this is soon to be joined by the Three Gorges Dam in China. The Itaipu Dam can generate the same amount of power as 12 nuclear power plants. The power generation of the Three Gorges Dam is expected to be higher, which will make it the largest hydroelectric power source in the world. Not all dams generate electricity. Most are built to provide irrigation water and flood control.

Dams on rivers create reservoirs, or large lakes, that store water until it is needed. The stored water is released through pipes that lead to turbines deep inside the dam. The falling water moves the turbines, which drive generators. The taller the dam, the farther the water falls and the more electricity produced. When there is excess electricity, water can be pumped back up into the reservoir so it can be released when there is a high electricity demand. Hydroelectric power is very efficient—about 90 percent of the water's energy is converted into electricity.

The Hoover Dam, on the Colorado River, supplies electricity to Las Vegas, which is rapidly expanding and has a high electricity consumption.

DISCUSS   Three Gorges Dam—Good or Bad?

When it is fully operational in 2011, the Three Gorges Dam is set to be the largest hydroelectric dam in the world, producing twice as much power as the Itaipu Dam in Brazil. It will create a reservoir 600 km (373 miles) long. The dam's capacity will be 17 million kilowatts, and its projected annual power generation is 84 billion **kWh**. It will supply power mainly to central China. This controversial project has attracted attention from around the world. It has both advantages and disadvantages. Some advantages are:

- Power generation. The dam will increase China's electricity output to ensure sufficient power for China's rapidly growing industries.
- Flood prevention. The dam will prevent flooding, which in the past has killed thousands and left millions homeless.
- Cleaner electricity. Hydroelectricity is cleaner than electricity produced by burning coal and 75 percent of China's electricity comes from coal-fired power plants. The electricity from the project will reduce the need to burn more coal, which will reduce emissions of sulfur and carbon dioxide.

Some disadvantages are:

- It is estimated that the reservoir will partially or completely flood more than 600 km² (262 miles²) of land, including two cities. As many as 4 million people will have to be rehoused.
- The dam and reservoir will alter the area's entire ecological system and environment. It will divert the Yangtze River's natural course and flood a vast area of land that is home to many species.
- Large quantities of silt will be dumped in the reservoir. Normally, the silt is dumped lower down the river, creating fertile flood plains.

Sluices are opened to divert flood water at the Three Gorges Dam near Yichang in central China's Hubei Province. The Three Gorges Dam is reported to have successfully controlled one of the biggest **flood crests** on the Yangtze River.

Wave Energy

Winds blowing across the surface of the ocean create waves. The energy from the movement of the waves can be harnessed to produce electricity. There are two main types of wave energy generation devices: fixed and floating.

FIXED DEVICES

Fixed generating devices are usually located on the seabed or the coast. One fixed device is called the Oscillating Water Column. Waves enter at the bottom of the column and force the air within the column through a turbine. Pressure increases within the column. As the wave retreats, the air is drawn back past the turbine due to the reduced air pressure on the ocean side of the turbine.

Another type of fixed device known as the TAPCHAN, or tapered channel system, is similar to that used in hydroelectric power plants. It consists of a channel connected to a reservoir in a cliff. This channel gets steadily narrower, causing the waves to increase in height. Eventually, the waves are high enough to pour over the walls, into the reservoir. The stored water is then fed through a turbine. Unfortunately, TAPCHAN systems are not suitable for all coastal regions.

A TAPCHAN system can only be used where there are consistent waves and a tidal range of less than 1 meter (3 ft.).

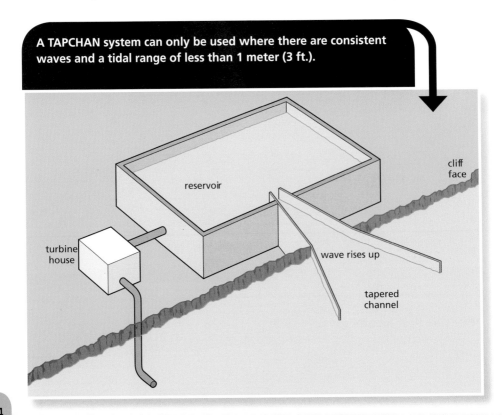

cliff face

reservoir

turbine house

wave rises up

tapered channel

A prototype wave-power generator was installed on the coast of Islay, Scotland, in 2000. As water enters and leaves a partly submerged chamber, the air above the water is compressed and decompressed. The forced air then drives a turbine. It can produce enough electricity to supply local villages. The first wave-power generator is due to be completed on the Isle of Lewis, Scotland, in 2009.

FLOATING DEVICES

Floating wave energy devices generate electricity when they rise and fall with the motion of the waves. One design, known as Pelamis, has 10 floating tubes placed end to end, forming a flexible tube 120 meters (394 ft.) long. Each tube moves up and down independently. This movement drives pumps that produce electricity. Floating devices have a number of other different designs, including Salter Duck, Clam, and the Archimedes Wave Swing. All have had limited success, but none has been used on a commercial scale yet.

The tidal barrage across the Rance River in France generates electricity for local towns. There is an 8-meter (26-ft.) difference in height between low tide and high tide.

Tidal Energy

A tidal barrage is a huge, damlike structure built across an **estuary**, with a series of **sluice gates** and turbines at the base. When the tide rises, water fills the estuary, pushes through the turbines, and becomes trapped behind the dam. When the tide falls, the water passes through in the opposite direction, turning the turbines again.

There are a number of barrages around the world. The Rance barrage in France makes use of an 8-meter (26-ft.) tidal range and can generate 11 gigawatts. The barrage built in the Bay of Fundy in Canada has a range of up to 16 meters (53 ft.) and can generate 29 gigawatts. There are also large barrages off the coast of China, which were built to replace coal-fired power plants.

Environmental Damage: Pros and Cons

Dams built across a river or an estuary and tidal barrages have severe environmental implications because they interfere with the flow of water. Dams on rivers create reservoirs that flood large areas of land. For example, the Balbina Dam in Brazil flooded 2,400 km² (926 miles²) of rain forest.

Water entering a reservoir dumps its silt. This causes a buildup of silt in the reservoir, which eventually has to be dredged. Normally, this silt would be dumped on the river's flood plain, providing a source of nutrients for the soil. The capacity of Lake Nasser, behind the Aswan Dam on the Nile River in Egypt, has been severely reduced by silt. Downstream from the dam, the river transports less than 10 percent of its normal load of silt. This means that less silt reaches the Nile Delta, which is now being eroded. In addition, Nile Valley farmers must increasingly rely on artificial fertilizers instead of silt.

Another problem is that silt increases the nutrient content of reservoir water. Algae use the nutrients and rapidly increase in number, producing an algal bloom over the surface of the water. As the algae die, they are decomposed by bacteria. This increases the number of bacteria, which use up the oxygen in the water. The lack of oxygen causes fish and other organisms in the water to die.

Tidal barrages reduce tidal range, so there are no extreme low or high tides. Low-lying mudflats and salt marshes could become permanently flooded, resulting in a loss of habitat for wading birds, which are abundant in estuarine areas. The flush time—the time it takes for water to move out of an estuary—could increase, causing pollutants in the water to remain there for longer before draining out and being diluted in the open sea. The salt concentration could decrease and harm marine organisms. However, some biologists believe that some of these changes could lead to an increase in the number of different types of invertebrate species. There would be more food for birds, but the birds may be different from the ones there now. Do you think the cons outweigh the pros?

Lake Moogerah in Queensland, Australia, was created by damming a river. The newly formed lake has flooded a rain forest. The remains of the trees can still be seen.

HEAT FROM THE GROUND

Earth is still cooling down from the time it was formed, and its **core** is like an energy store. **Geothermal** power uses energy generated from within Earth's core. In volcanic areas, such as Iceland, New Zealand, and parts of the United States, hot rocks lie close to Earth's surface. The heat warms the surface waters, creating hot springs. In addition, the Sun heats surface layers of the ground.

New Zealand's North Island has several hot springs such as this one, Whakarewarewa Thermal Reserve. The hot springs have been created by water passing over the hot rocks before coming to the surface.

Tapping the Hot Water

Geothermal heat can be used in two ways. One method is simply to pump out hot water and use it to heat buildings or to produce steam to generate electricity. Geothermal power plants are built close to hot springs, so they can use the natural source of steam to spin their turbines. The world's largest geothermal power plant is The Geysers, near San Francisco, California. This power plant can produce much of the electricity needed by the city. More than 250 wells have been drilled into the rocks, and they carry steam directly from the ground into the power plant. Some of the deepest wells reach nearly 4 km (2.5 miles) into the earth. In modern geothermal plants, once the water has cooled down it is pumped back into the ground to replace the water that was extracted. Water is reheated by the hot rocks near Earth's surface.

The second method makes use of hot, dry rocks. Pressurized cold water is pumped through a borehole into hot rocks that are highly fractured. The cold water seeps through the cracks in these hot rocks and is heated by them. Then, the hot water is pumped up to the surface through a second borehole. Prototypes have been built, but this method has not been used on a commercial scale. One of the problems is preventing a high-pressure, high-temperature **blowout**.

The waste water from this geothermal power plant in Iceland is still warm. It is used to heat the Blue Lagoon, a popular recreational pool.

In Iceland, underground heating pipes along the streets ensure that the roads are ice-free all year. Here, new heating pipes are being laid in a street in Iceland's capital city, Reykjavik.

Environmental Impact

Although geothermal energy is a superclean energy source, it must be used properly to prevent possible environmental damage. New geothermal systems reinject water into the earth after its heat is used. This helps to preserve the resource. Care must be taken in planning geothermal projects to ensure that they do not cool nearby hot springs or cause intermixing with groundwater. Geothermal projects can produce some carbon dioxide emissions, but these are a fraction of those produced by the cleanest fossil fuel power plants of the same size.

Ground Heat

The temperature of the ground is remarkably constant throughout the year. Although there may be temperature variations in the top layer of soil, deeper down the temperature stays the same year-round, approximately 6°C (43°F). Ground heat pumps can be used to provide heating and air-conditioning in homes. These pumps are highly efficient and make use of the temperature difference between the air and the ground. In the winter, heat is removed from the ground and transferred into a building or home to keep it warm. In the summer, heat is transferred from the building or home to keep it cool and is pumped into the ground. In either cycle, water can be heated for other purposes, such as bathing or cooking.

The heat pump unit takes the place of a boiler inside the home or building. In a typical installation, a loop of plastic pipe is either laid along a long horizontal trench in the ground, or placed in a nearby vertical drill hole that may reach down 30 meters (99 ft.) or more. Then the hole is filled with clay. A water-antifreeze solution is circulated through the loop and the heat pump. In winter, cold solution passes along the pipe and picks up heat from the ground. When it enters the home or buidling, it is several degrees warmer. In summer the hot air in the house heats up the solution, which enters the loop in the ground, where it loses its heat. A cooler solution then returns to the home or buidling. More than 100,000 heat pumps have been installed in buildings in the United States.

"We've had a fourfold increase in interest [in geothermal systems] over the past four years ... Prices vary, but for economy of operation, geothermal wins hands down."

Duwayne Marks, director of energy efficiency for Virginia Power.

NUCLEAR ENERGY

Nuclear power is produced by splitting atoms. All matter is made up of tiny particles called atoms. Each atom consists of a **nucleus** made of protons and neutrons surrounded by electrons. When the nucleus of a large atom is split in two, energy is released. This is called nuclear fission.

There are currently about 440 nuclear power plants around the world. Together, they generate approximately 15 percent of the world's electricity. Nuclear power generation is clean, but there are major concerns about its safety and cost. The metal uranium is used as fuel (its atoms are split). Only a tiny amount or uranium is needed, because 500 grams (15.5 ounces) of this metal produces the same quantity of heat as 1,400 metric tons of coal.

Fission Reactions

The uranium atom is large and unstable. Its instability means that neutrons are given off by the nucleus. These neutrons are fast-moving and may bump into other uranium atoms, causing them to split and release heat energy. This sets off a chain reaction, with nucleus after nucleus splitting. When this occurs, vast amounts of energy are released. However, this chain reaction has to be controlled, or a massive explosion will result. This is exactly what happened in early atomic bombs. Fission reactions can be controlled if some of the neutrons are absorbed.

FOCUS Nuclear Reactors

Nuclear fission takes place inside a **reactor** that is surrounded by a thick layer of concrete or steel. One of the more advanced designs of a nuclear power plant is the advanced gas-cooled reactor. Uranium is spread out in thin fuel rods and lowered into the reactor. Between the fuel rods are control rods made of a material called boron, which absorbs neutrons. By lowering and raising the control rods, it is possible to control the chain reaction. If the control rods are lowered, more neutrons are absorbed, and the chain reaction slows down. Both the fuel and control rods are surrounded by a moderator. This is a substance, such as graphite, that does not change during the reactions but helps to slow down the neutrons. Carbon dioxide gas is pumped around the reactor to take up heat from the reaction within the reactor. The hot carbon dioxide is used to heat water to produce steam.

Is Nuclear Power Safe?

There are major problems with nuclear power. When uranium atoms split, they produce smaller particles, which are **radioactive**. These radioactive particles can cause cancer and even death. Therefore, a thick layer of concrete or lead around a reactor is essential to prevent these particles from entering the environment. However, once the uranium is used up, the fuel rods have to be replaced. Used fuel rods are highly radioactive, as are the control rods. The reactor has a life of up to 50 years, after which it can no longer be used. Careful disposal is needed for all of these radioactive materials, but there are no guaranteed safe disposal methods. These materials are so dangerous that they have to be buried in special containers in the ground for hundreds of years.

Another risk is the threat from radiation leakage during an accident. A major nuclear accident occurred at the Chernobyl nuclear reactor in the Ukraine on April 26, 1986. Two explosions produced a huge radioactive cloud that spread across Europe. To prevent more leaks, the entire reactor plant was encased in concrete (shown right). Since that time, more than 125,000 people may have died prematurely as a result of exposure to Chernobyl radiation. High-energy radioactive particles can pass deep into the body, where they can damage or kill cells. Exposure to a large dose of radiation will kill a large number of cells. The long-term damage can include cancer. Cancer is caused by cells dividing uncontrollably. This abnormal growth of cells is called a tumor. Damage to cells in the reproductive system can cause birth defects in children, such as missing limbs and brain damage.

Nuclear Fusion

A process called nuclear fusion powers the Sun. The high temperature of the Sun causes small nuclei to collide into each other with such force that they fuse to form one heavier nucleus. At the same time, energy is released.

Scientists are hoping that the next generation of nuclear power plants will be powered by nuclear fusion. The fuel will be heavy hydrogen (called deuterium), and the waste material will be water. When two nuclei of heavy hydrogen fuse, their combined masses are slightly less than the mass of the original particles. This tiny amount represents the energy. The energy can be harnessed and used to generate electricity.

The problem is that the fuel has to be heated to temperatures of up to 100 million°C (212 million°F) and has to be contained by very powerful magnets. Scientists have built small prototype reactors and have even made the nuclei fuse in a short, self-sustaining, controlled fusion reaction. But it only worked for a few seconds and used far more energy than was released by the fusion. To make electricity commercially, a fusion reactor will have to work consistently for decades. Although fusion reactors will solve many of the world's energy problems, a commercial reactor will probably not be available for many decades, and the cost will be high. However, as concerns about global warming grow and oil supplies dry up, the need for a clean and plentiful energy source such as this is urgent.

The experimental Tokamak fusion reactor has powerful magnets. The magnetic field squeezes hot **plasma** into a very small space and brings deuterium and tritium together so that they can fuse.

The Hydrogen Bomb

The two atomic bombs dropped on Japan at the end of World War II were based on a fission reaction. Atomic bombs contain uranium or plutonium, which is split to release vast amounts of energy and radioactive particles. The hydrogen bomb (also known as a thermonuclear bomb) is different. It relies on the fusion reaction, and its fuel is a special form of hydrogen. The fusion reaction begins when hydrogen is subjected to incredibly high temperatures. The explosion of a hydrogen bomb creates an extremely hot zone near its center, which **vaporizes** nearly all matter present to form a gas at extremely high pressure. Then, a destructive shock wave travels outward. Exceptionally high temperatures are required to start a fusion reaction. The high temperatures are created by the explosion of a small fission bomb, which releases some radioactivity. Scientists are trying to control this type of fusion reaction to generate electricity.

The first thermonuclear explosion took place in 1952 at Eniwetok Atoll in the South Pacific. The explosion created a mushroom cloud above the island.

BIOPOWER

Each year, plants trap enough energy to meet the world's demands up to eight times over. But only a fraction of this energy is utilized. Plants represent a renewable source of energy. Wood is the world's oldest and most common form of **bioenergy**. The supply of wood can be maintained, if more trees are planted after they are harvested. However, this will not create the same habitat for other species. In many parts of the less economically developed world, wood is being burned faster than it is being replaced. Fortunately, there are many other plants that can be grown on a large scale to provide energy.

Biofuels

Biofuels are produced either from plants that are grown especially for fuel, or from plant wastes. Straw, a plant waste, is left over after harvesting cereal crops. It can be used as a fuel in power plants or processed to produce a fuel for cars, a second-generation biofuel.

Willow is a fast-growing plant. It is left for four or five years, then the shoots are cut back down to ground level and allowed to regrow.

In Denmark straw-fired power plants provide about two percent of the country's electricity needs. Hungary plans to have completed the world's largest straw-fired power plant by 2010.

Energy crops are plants grown just to generate energy. The plants, such as willow, sugarcane, bananas, and *Miscanthus* (a tall, bamboo-like grass), are fast-growing and can be harvested within a short time. Their energy content is approximately half that of coal and one-third that of oil. Grasses are harvested annually, while willow is harvested at intervals of four or five years. Sugarcane and *Miscanthus* grow to heights of up to 3 meters (10 ft.) in a single season. The woody stems are harvested at the end of the growing season, and new shoots appear the following spring. Willow plants are cut down to a stump and left to regrow. Approximately 40 hectares (99 acres) of willow will generate power for thousands of homes.

 FOCUS **Oil Crops and Genetic Modification**

Many industrial oils come from fossil fuels or expensive chemical processes. It is possible that oil crops may be genetically modified to give them the ability to make oils with specific industrial uses. This would involve finding the gene responsible for making a particular oil in an organism, removing the gene from the organism's **DNA**, and inserting it into the DNA of the crop plant. For example, petroselinic acid is a compound used in the manufacture of detergents, plastics, and nylon. The coriander plant produces this substance, but coriander cannot be grown as an oil crop. If the gene that makes this compound in coriander is identified, it could be transferred to the rapeseed plant. The modified rapeseed plant could then be grown and processed for this chemical.

Genetic engineering could make the rapeseed plant produce oils suitable for industrial use.

Powering Cars

Many crops produce oils that can be used to fuel cars. This fuel is called biodiesel. Different oil crops around the world can be used, such as rapeseed in Europe and North America, coconut oil in the Philippines, sunflower oil in South Africa, and palm and castor oil in Brazil.

Another fuel derived from plants is ethanol. It is produced from organic waste and from crops such as sugarcane, sugar beet, and corn. The Clean Air Act of 1990 requires that gasoline sold in polluted cities in the United States be at least two percent oxygen by weight, which ensures complete **combustion** of fuel when it burns, especially when an engine is cold. It also reduces the level of pollutants such as carbon monoxide.

Biodiesel is gasoline that has been modified by adding either six percent ethanol by volume or 11 percent of an additive called MTBE. For a while, MTBE was the preferred option of the oil companies. But recently it was discovered that MTBE is contaminating water sources across the United States. It is soluble in water, and once in water it breaks down very slowly. As a result, there is a growing interest in ethanol as a fuel.

This ethanol plant on the Colorado plains in the United States turns corn into ethanol, a renewable fuel source.

Gasohol is another fuel that contains ethanol. Gasohol is 80 to 90 percent petroleum spirit and 10 to 20 per centethanol. A gallon of gasohol produces less air pollution than a gallon of gasoline. Gasohol makes up 24 percent of the market in Brazil. Sugarcane is grown extensively in Brazil, so there is a ready supply of ethanol. However, gasohol costs more than normal gasoline and has to be subsidized.

The various fuels available at this pump include gas petrol liquid, electricity, bioethanol, biodiesel, and hydrogen.

DISCUSS   Biofuels—Help or Hindrance?

Biofuels could reduce the world's greenhouse gas emissions. They are carbon-neutral because they take up carbon dioxide while they are growing and release it when they are burned. Biofuel emissions could be less than half those of fossil fuels. However, energy is used to grow and process biofuel crops, and there are environmental concerns about the loss of habitats and the effects large-scale farming has on biodiversity. In Southeast Asia, rain forests are cleared to make way for new palm oil plantations. In Brazil, rain forests give way to fields of sugarcane and soy. More of the world's cereals, such as corn and soy, are also being used to make fuel rather than food. This creates shortages that push food prices up around the world. The best approach may be to use plant wastes, such as straw, to produce second-generation biofuels.

"Biofuels are rapidly becoming the main cause of deforestation in countries like Indonesia, Malaysia, and Brazil. We call it deforestation diesel."

Simone Lovera, managing coordinator of the Global Forest Coalition

Biogas

Biogas is a gas that is produced when animal and plant wastes rot. Bacteria ferment the waste under anaerobic (oxygen-free) conditions. The products of this fermentation include carbon dioxide and methane.

Methane is produced in landfills, where the buried waste decays and generates this gas. Often, methane is allowed to escape into the atmosphere. However, it could be collected and piped to local industries where it can be burned to release heat.

Biogas can also be produced under more controlled conditions in pits in the ground or in tanks called biogas digesters. All forms of human and animal waste can be added to the digester. The rotting mass releases gases, such as methane, that can be piped away and burned as a fuel for heating and cooking.

A wide range of waste materials, such as animal dung, can be added to a biogas digester. The resulting gas can be used for heating and cooking in the home.

Biogas is a major fuel in many less economically developed countries, where almost every rural family or village could make use of a biogas digester to generate fuel. Biogas digesters can be used on farms to dispose of animal wastes, too. The biogas can be used to power a generator to produce electricity.

Intensive farming in Denmark and the Netherlands generates a large amount of animal waste, which needs careful disposal. It is fermented in digesters to produce biogas, while the residue is used as a fertilizer. Elsewhere, household and animal wastes are burned in specially modified power plants, rather than being used to make biogas. These power plants have to meet strict emission controls to prevent the release of toxic chemicals.

This train in Sweden runs on biogas.

THE FUTURE OF RENEWABLE SOURCES

In 2006 renewable energy sources accounted for less than 20 percent of all energy sources. Most of this energy came from biofuels, mainly wood, with only five percent coming from other renewable sources. Over the next century, it is likely that this will change, with most of the energy coming from renewable sources and only a fraction from fossil fuels. Renewable energy source manufacturers will need to conform to the increasingly strict emission requirements of many countries.

New technological developments will be needed to ensure that the energy conversions are as efficient as possible. As well as the energy sources identified in this book, it will be necessary to find others. One source that has been mostly disregarded is deep water.

Looking to the Oceans

Oceans cover two-thirds of Earth's surface. They range in depth from just a few meters to several kilometers. Many of the deeper parts of the oceans have not yet been explored.

Vast underwater kelp forests are found off the California coast. These seaweeds grow rapidly and could be used as a source of energy.

Forests of seaweed lie in the shallow waters off many coasts and are a potential source of energy. Harvesting seaweed is not a new concept. It is used as a food, fed to animals, and spread on fields as a natural fertilizer. But it is not yet used as a fuel. Fast-growing seaweeds called kelp can be grown as a crop and then harvested. Giant kelp can grow up to 1 metre (3 ft.) in height a day! In a trial experiment, kelp was farmed in the sea off California. It was harvested and used to make methane gas. Kelp digesters that produce methane may one day become common in many coastal towns around the world.

FOCUS   Ocean Thermal Energy Conversion

Within the 30° latitude on both sides of the equator, there is a thermocline in the ocean. This means there is a temperature difference between the surface water and deeper water. The temperature of the surface layer of water is 25°C (77°F), while the water at a depth of 1,000 meters (3,282 ft.) is only 5°C (41°F). The warm surface water can be used to evaporate liquids with a low boiling point, such as chlorofluorocarbons (CFCs) and ammonia. This produces a vapor that can be used to drive a turbine attached to a generator. Cold seawater passing through a condenser turns the vapor back to liquid to restart the system.

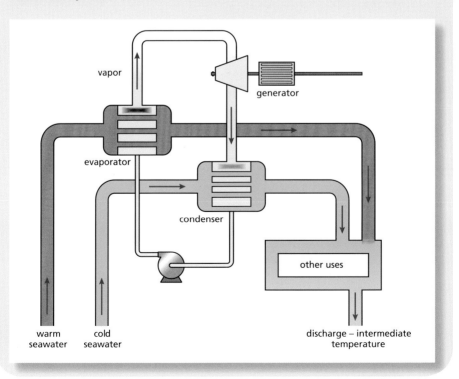

vapor

generator

evaporator

condenser

other uses

warm seawater   cold seawater

discharge – intermediate temperature

Tidal Barrages and Underwater Wind Farms

Tidal barrages can be an effective way to generate power, and there are many sites in the world where they could be built. One of the best sites in the world is the Severn Estuary in the United Kingdom. Although there is a plan to develop a barrage across the estuary, it has not yet been approved. However, large tidal barrages have a harmful effect on the wildlife in an estuary. As an alternative, engineers are studying the powerful underwater currents that run along many coasts.

Offshore wind farms, such as the Middelgrunden wind farm (see page 20) are built in shallow waters, so the turbines are above the water. In the future wind generators could disappear under the ocean. These underwater wind farms would be built in places where the currents are strong. The flow of water, not wind, would turn the blades and power the turbine. Potentially, a single turbine could produce enough power to supply a small village. Water currents are far more reliable than the wind. However, turbines could not just be placed anywhere. They could not be located along shipping routes or areas of nature conservation, and would need to be in water deep enough to cover the blades, but near enough to the shore for cables to carry electricity.

 FOCUS **Marine Methane**

Scientists have discovered that there is enough methane gas lying on the seabed to keep the world supplied with energy for hundreds of years. This methane was produced by bacteria feeding on the remains of dead plants and animals. The cold waters of the deep oceans caused the methane to freeze, and it now lies scattered in tiny crystals over the seabed. Accessing this source of energy is difficult. One way to collect the methane may be to pump steam down a pipe onto the seabed. The heat would melt the crystals, turning the methane back to gas. The gas could be trapped in an underwater balloon and towed by submarine to docks for storage. Methane, however, is a type of fossil fuel and is not a renewable source of energy.

Grain silos, such as these in Nebraska, are built close to the fields where cereal crops are grown. In the future the silos could be replaced by biorefineries that will process the crops.

Biorefineries

Today, oil refineries take crude oil and break it down into parts that can then be used for a wide range of materials, including plastics. In the future refineries will have to use more crops. Oil refineries could be replaced by "green" biorefineries. Instead of oil, crops would be processed into plastics, chemicals, and fuels. One grain manufacturer in Nebraska has already built a factory where crops go in and a whole range of products comes out, including polyactic acid used in plastics for clothing, food containers, and cling film. "Green" plastics can be made from corn and wheat, while rapeseed and soybeans could be used to make biodiesel.

Mobile Power

Fuel cells will play an increasingly important role in storing and releasing energy. However, current fuel cell models are heavy and bulky. Research is under way to produce tiny fuel cells that will be small enough to power laptops and cell phones. These fuel cells will have to be light, easy to recharge, and last a long time. The aim is to produce a fuel cell that runs for 12 hours and can be recharged with a small amount of liquid fuel.

The most promising fuel cell design is the direct methanol fuel cell, which runs on a mix of two percent methanol in water. First, the methanol is converted to carbon dioxide and hydrogen. Normally this reaction can only take place at high temperatures. However, the presence of a platinum **catalyst** allows the reaction to take place at low temperatures. Then, the hydrogen reacts with oxygen. This process has been made even more efficient and economical by using platinum nanoparticles.

CONCLUSION

People will continue to burn fossil fuels as long as they are available at a cheaper cost than other alternatives. Fortunately, antipollution technology can reduce some of the pollutants released from burning these fuels, but this does not always include greenhouse gases. In the future many new sources of energy will be needed. They will have to both replace fossil fuels and supply the extra energy needs of a growing world population.

Rising Cost and Demand

The world's population is growing rapidly. In economically developing countries, such as China and India, many people are achieving greater wealth. This leads to higher standards of living, more people owning cars, and an increase in energy demands. Energy demands in wealthy industrial countries also continue to grow.

Another problem is the soaring cost of generating electricity. In 2000 it cost about $1 billion to build a typical power plant in the United States. This cost has now risen to $2.3 billion, mostly due to the increasing cost of building materials, especially steel and cement. The cost of building wind farms and solar power plants has also risen.

These solar-powered, hot-water cylinders in Australia provide a high-tech solution to a household need.

Is Energy Efficiency the Answer?

With both building costs and energy demands at an all-time high, many feel the answer lies in energy efficiency. A program of energy efficiency measures could reduce the need to build new power plants. Legislation could be put in place to ensure that electrical appliances, especially air-conditioning units, are more energy efficient, households could replace traditional lightbulbs with energy efficient ones, and new building standards could improve the heating efficiency of homes and offices.

Promising Alternatives

As fossil fuels become rarer, governments may look again at nuclear energy. Nuclear fission will still be at the heart of many nuclear power plants, but developments in technology mean that these power plants will be much safer than current ones. Within 50 years, it is also possible that the first commercial fusion power plant could be in operation.

However, there is a better option—fuel cells. These can be likened to a highly efficient engine with no moving parts. Whenever power is used, fuel cells can be used as an alternative, from powering cell phones and laptops to generating electricity on a commercial scale. Potentially, fuel cells could replace every battery and combustion engine in the world. At the moment, fuel cells are expensive, costing thousands of dollars per kilowatt of power, compared with hundreds of dollars per kilowatt for a gas turbine power plant. However, if the cells are produced in large quantities, the price will fall, and in time the cost will be comparable with and possibly cheaper than conventional power sources. Engineers will have to redesign cars and other objects in order to use fuel cells. It is even possible that, one day, everyone may have their own personal power plant, based on a fuel cell that provides all their needs for powering cars and homes.

Energy Crisis

At the moment most electricity is supplied by large central power plants that feed electricity into a national power grid. Often, fossil fuels used to power the plants are imported. Power plants cause more pollution and are less efficient than some newer energy sources. People will have to learn to depend on a variety of energy sources, with each source generating energy on a small scale. Advances in energy technology are being made all the time, but some scientists argue that there will come a time when the demand for energy outstrips the supply.

TIMELINE

1500   **1600**

The Dutch improve on the design of windmills and use the new windmills for grinding grain.

1908

William Bailey of the Carnegie Steel Company invents a solar collector with an insulated box and copper coils. By the end of World War I, more than 4,000 have been sold.

1895

Two men buy the rights to Kemp's solar system. High gas and coal prices create demand, and by 1897 they have fitted 30 percent of homes in Pasadena, California, with solar water heaters.

1940

More than 6 million wind-powered water pumps are used in the United States, mainly for pumping water and generating electricity.

1941

A 1.25-megawatt wind turbine is hooked to the Central Vermont Public Service grid near Rutland, Vermont.

1942

The first experimental nuclear power plant is built at the University of Chicago.

Denmark links a 200-kilowatt wind turbine to its national power grid.

1990

In the United States, the Clean Air Act requires gasoline sold in polluted cities to be at least two percent oxygen by weight.

1984

Tax credits lead to the commercial development of wind power in California. During this period 6,870 turbines are installed.

1994

The cost of wind power falls and becomes competitive with many other power generators.

2000

More than 3,800 megawatts of new wind energy generating capacity are brought online worldwide. The global wind power capacity rises to 17,300 megawatts, enough to generate 37 billion kWh of electricity each year.

1767

The Swiss scientist Horace de Saussure builds the world's first solar collector, which is used by Sir John Herschel to cook food during his expedition to South Africa in the 1830s.

1839

Sir William Grove, a British scientist, writes the first known account of the fuel cell.

1891

Inventor Clarence Kemp patents the first commercial solar water heater in the United States.

1854

A wind-powered water pump is introduced in the United States. It is a fan type, with **vanes** around a wheel, and a tail to keep it pointed into the wind.

1952

The first hydrogen bomb is exploded on Eniwetok in the South Pacific by the United States.

1954

Bell Telephone researchers discover the sensitivity of a silicon wafer to sunlight, and the solar cell is developed.

1956

The first commercial nuclear power plant opens at Calder Hall in Cumbria in the United Kingdom.

1982

The world's first solar power plant, Solar One, located near Barstow, California, starts to generate electricity.

1973

Oil prices rise dramatically. There are further shortages when Arab oil exporting countries set up an oil **embargo**. The oil shortages persuade governments to set up programs to develop alternative energy sources, such as wind and solar power.

2001

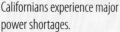

Californians experience major power shortages.

The world's largest offshore wind farm opens near Copenhagen, Denmark.

2004

A solar program launched by California Governor Arnold Schwarzenegger aims to have 1 million solar roofs in California, by 2017.

2011

The world's largest hydroelectric power plant project, the Three Gorges Dam in China, is expected to become fully operational.

GLOSSARY

acid rain rain that has a pH of less than 5.5 due to weak acids and pollutants, such as nitrogen and sulfur oxides

bioenergy energy derived from plants, such as wood, grasses, and sugarcane

blowout sudden explosion of oil or water from the ground

catalyst chemical that enables reactions to take place more readily or at lower temperatures

combustion burning

composite material made of two or more substances

condense to change from gas or vapor to liquid

core central part

crude oil oil in its natural, raw state that has not yet been processed or refined

current flow or movement of electrically charged particles

DNA deoxyribonucleic acid; genetic material found in most cells

efficient measure of how much energy is usefully transferred as the form of energy wanted

electricity form of energy made up of charged particles that flow along a conductor, creating an electric current

electrochemical chemistry that involves electricity

electrode conductor through which electricity enters or leaves a substance. It is usually a wire or rod.

electrolyte substance that conducts electricity when molten or in a solution, such as acidified water

electromagnet soft iron core that is made into a magnet when electricity flows through a surrounding coil

embargo order by a government that prevents commercial activity

energy power, such as heat, electricity, or movement

estuary place where a river enters the ocean and freshwater meets saltwater

exhaust hot gases emitted by the engine of a vehicle

flood crest the maximum height of a flood wave as it passes a certain location

flywheel heavy wheel on a spinning shaft used to control machinery or store energy

fossil fuel fuel that forms in the Earth over millions of years from the remains of dead plants and animals. Coal, oil, and gas are all fossil fuels.

fuel cell device that converts energy. Electricity and heat are produced when the fuels within a fuel cell react together.

generator device that produces electrical energy

geothermal energy from Earth's hot core

gigawatt 1 billion watts

global warming process by which the average global temperature of Earth is gradually increasing

impermeable something that cannot be penetrated

kerosene type of fuel derived from oil, such as paraffin oil

kilowatt 1,000 watts

kinetic energy energy of a moving object

kWh kilowatt-hour, unit of energy often used to measure electrical energy use

megawatt 1 million watts

nucleus central part of an atom, made up of protons and neutrons

pH measure of the acidity or alkalinity of a solution

photovoltaic panel panel made up of many solar cells that can convert light energy into electricity using silicon

plasma gas of protons and neutrons

pollutant substance that contaminates the air, land, or water

radioactive property of a substance, which gives off subatomic particles

reactor area of a nuclear power plant where nuclear fission takes place

renewable describes energy sources that are naturally replaced and will not run out

satellite artificial body placed in orbit around Earth

semiconductor solid substance that becomes more conductive at higher temperatures

sluice gate sliding gate that controls the flow or volume of water

smog layer of fog and smoke mixed with air pollutants that can hang over a city. Photochemical smog is due to the chemical action of light on such pollutants.

solar power energy derived from the Sun

turbine machine that is used to change movement energy into mechanical energy

vane blade of a wind generator

vaporize to turn a liquid into a gas

FIND OUT MORE

Further Reading

Morgan, Sally. *From Windmills to Hydrogen Fuel Cells: Discovering Alternative Energy Sources*. Chicago: Heinemann Library, 2007.

Oxlade, Chris and Terry Jennings. *Energy*. Mankato, Minn.: Black Rabbit Books, 2009.

Royston, Angela. *Energy of the Future*. Chicago: Heinemann Library, 2008.

Snedden, Robert. *Energy Alternatives*. Chicago: Heinemann Library, 2006.

Solway, Andrew. *Harnessing the Sun's Energy*. Chicago: Heinemann Library, 2009.

Have a look for magazines that publish articles on alternative energy topics, such as *Popular Science, New Scientist, Science, Scientific American, International Wildlife*, and *People and the Planet*.

Websites

www.energy.gov/sciencetech/bioscience.htm
This web page from the Department of Energy describes the science behind different forms of energy.

www.eia.doe.gov/
This website contains official energy statistics for the United States for each of the different energy sources. It also forecasts future use and has a section on the environment, historical data, and other energy use in other countries.

www.pvpower.com
The Photovoltaic Power website has information on the technology, applications and history of photovoltaic power.

INDEX